Escape

Sarah Fleming

Contents

Definition:
escape:
1. to get free
2. to get away

Trackers

World War II

If soldiers were captured during World War II, they were sent to prisoner-of-war (POW) camps.

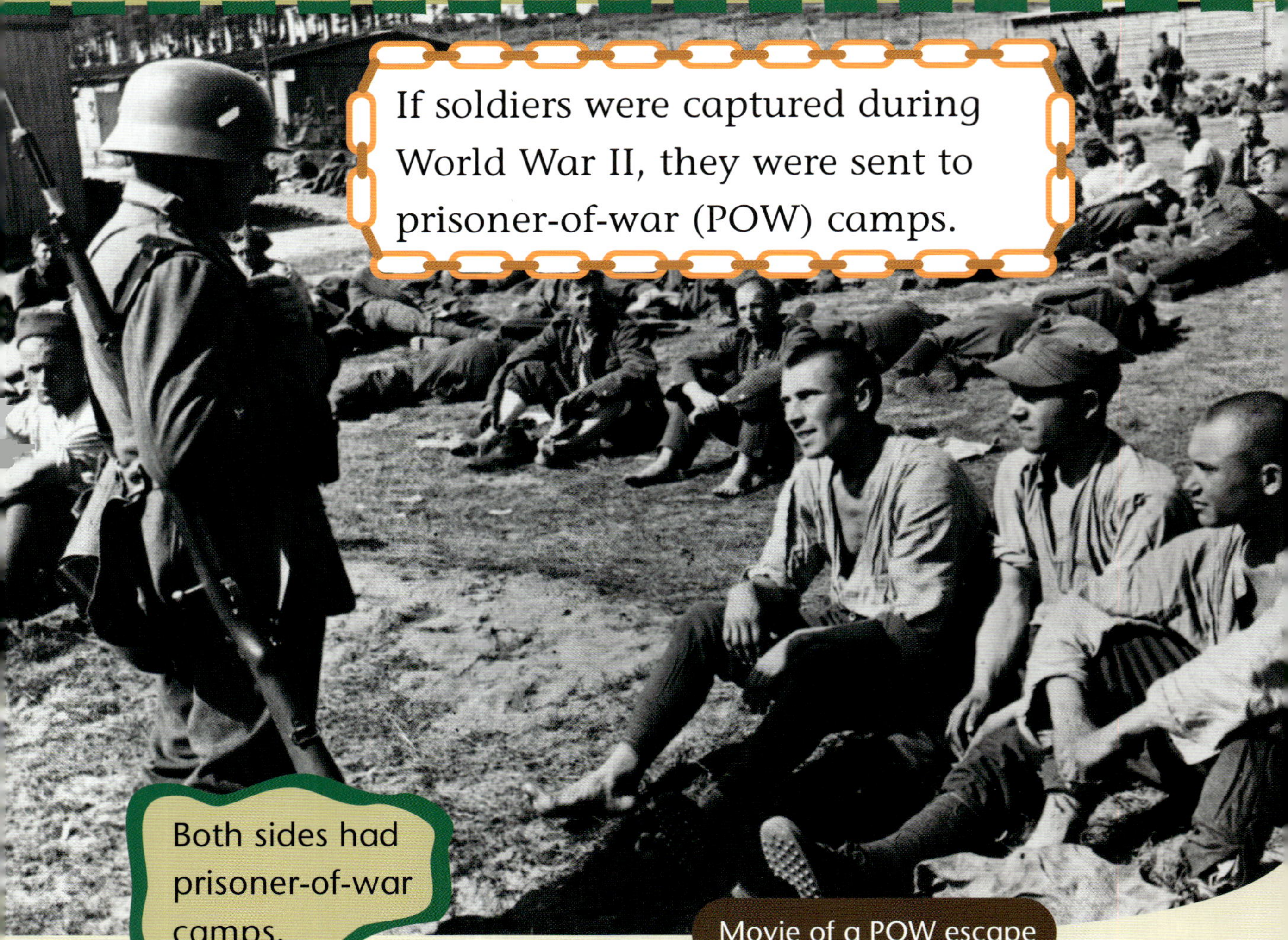

Both sides had prisoner-of-war camps.

Movie of a POW escape

Some prisoners tried to escape because they wanted to get home or start fighting again.

Definition: Nazis: members of the ruling political party in Germany, 1937–1945

Pat Reid was a British soldier who was caught by the **Nazis**. In 1940 he escaped from a prison camp by digging a tunnel from the camp under a road outside the camp.

Reid escaped dressed as a woman. He put some food into sacks across his chest. He shaved his legs and made a skirt out of a curtain. He wore a red spotted handkerchief on his head.

Reid walked 75 miles (120 km) in five days, but then he was caught again.

Many prisoners of war who escaped did not reach safety. Like Reid, they were caught again. They were all sent to Colditz, a prison for difficult prisoners from which there was supposedly no escape.

Colditz!

Colditz Castle was built on a rock. It had a high stone wall and lots of guards.

Reid finally escaped from Colditz in 1942. He and three other prisoners climbed into the prisoners' kitchen through a broken window. Then, they cut the bars off another window. They climbed through onto the roof of the guards' kitchen. They crawled along the roof and dropped to the ground.

They put socks over their shoes when they needed to be quiet!

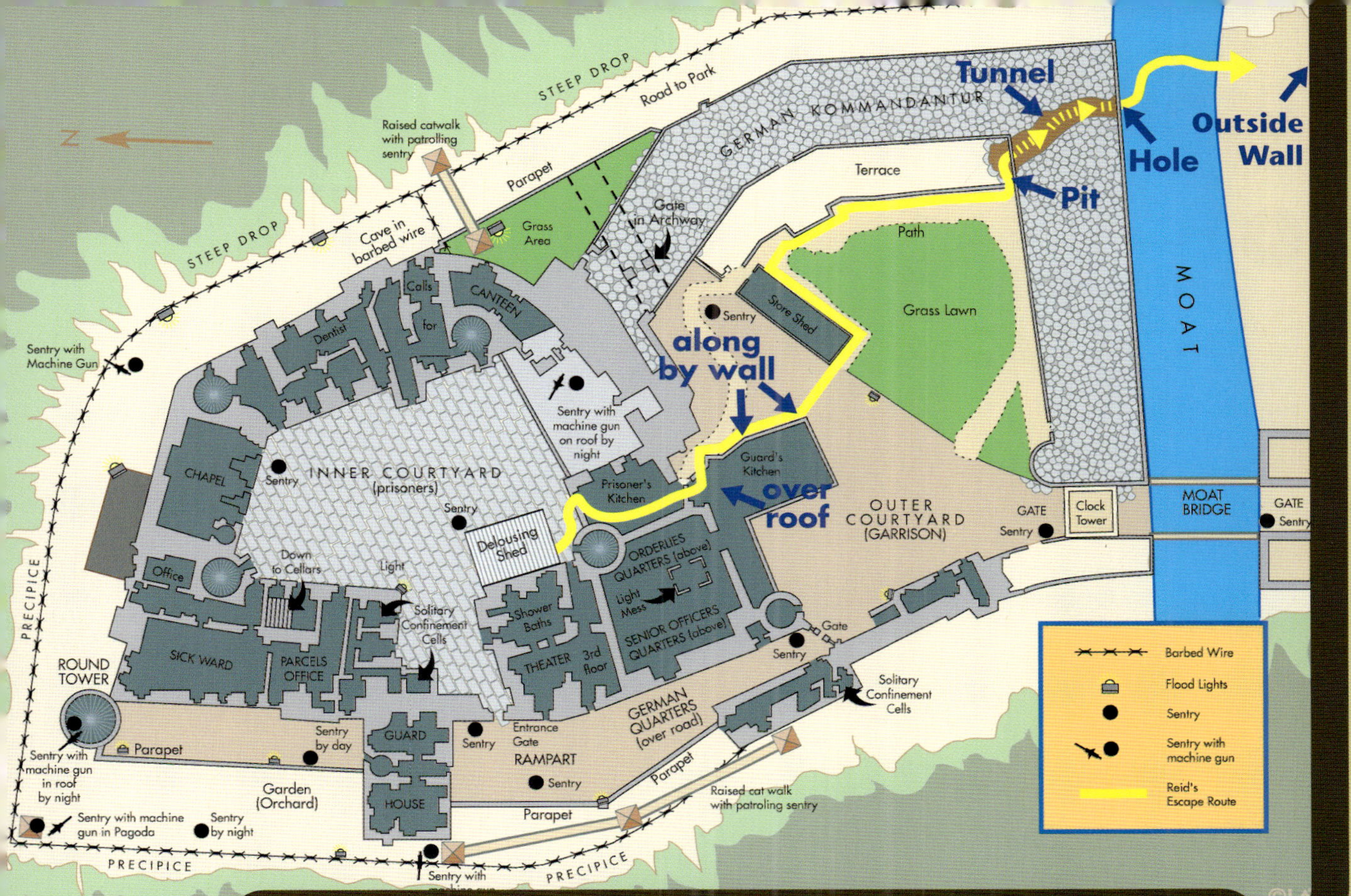

Plan of Colditz Castle, showing the route of Reid's successful escape

Next, they had to cross a floodlit courtyard, waiting until the guard had walked past. Then, they crept through a flower bed, jumped into a pit, went through a tunnel, squeezed through a hole, crossed the moat, and finally climbed over the outside wall, which had barbed wire running along the top of it.

They had escaped from Colditz, but they were still in Germany. They had to get to a safe country! It took them four more days of dodging soldiers before they finally crept into Switzerland during the night.

Other Escapes from Colditz

A As a woman

France

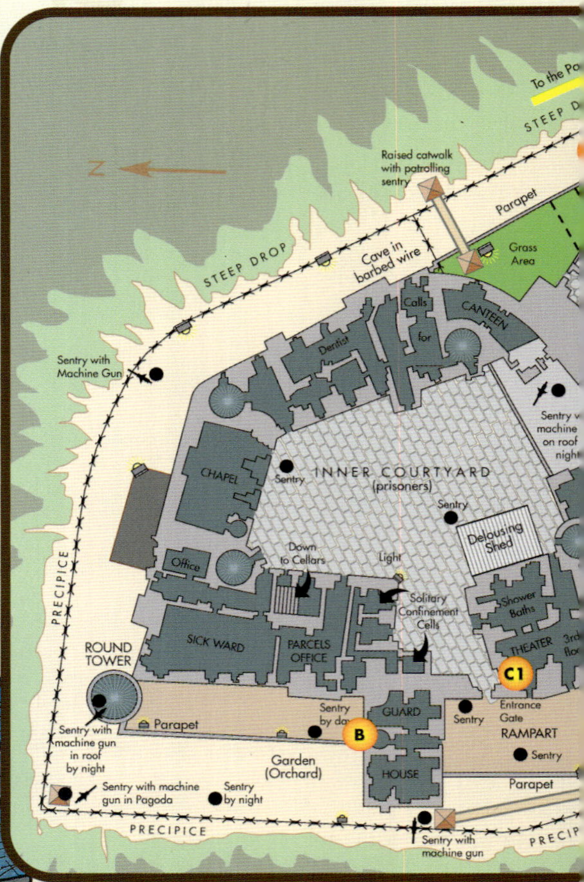

Poland

B Ropes made of sheets

Britain and Holland

C Under the stage, into the guards' area, and out through the main gate!

D Down a manhole

Holland

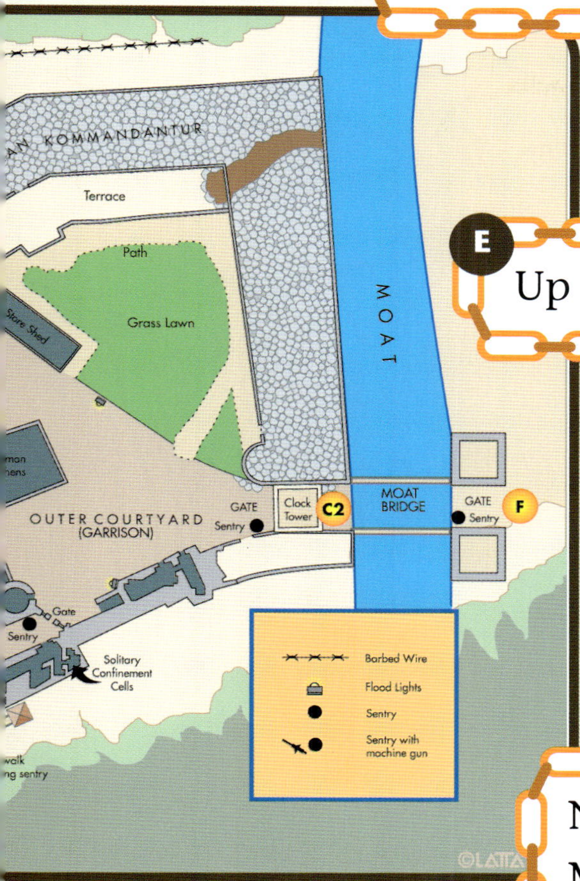

E Up and over

France

Not all of these prisoners escaped. Many were captured and brought back to Colditz. Thirty prisoners who escaped made it to safety.

Britain

F In a mattress

Prisoners who were brought back told other prisoners about things such as the land around the castle and where the train stations were. In this way, later prisoners had a better chance of escape. Yet each escape attempt made it more difficult for others because the Nazi guards became more careful.

Handy Hints for Escapers

Use floor covering to make belts.

Melt down lead to make buttons and medals.

Make keys out of iron bed parts.
Use blankets to make escape clothes, such as fake German uniforms.
Take wood from anywhere (bed slats, floorboards) to support the walls and ceilings of escape tunnels.

Locks

The locks at Colditz were very hard to **pick**.

Definition: pick: to unlock a lock without the keys

Locks have been made for thousands of years to keep people from getting in or out of places, or getting to private things.

Locks have also been made for people to wear, to keep them from escaping.

American prisoners were sent to work tied together with one chain. They were called a "chain gang."

Slaves were put in chains to keep them from escaping.

This is an excerpt from the 1837 diary of a slave named Charles Ball.

"A strong iron collar was closely fitted by means of a padlock around each of our necks. A chain of iron, about a hundred feet in length, was passed through the hasp of each padlock. In addition to this, we were handcuffed in pairs, with iron staples and bolts, with a short chain, about a foot long, uniting the handcuffs and their wearers in pairs."

Alcatraz

From 1934 to 1963, the rocky island of Alcatraz was made into a prison to hold the most difficult prisoners in the United States. Only thirty-six prisoners ever tried to escape, and most of those were killed or drowned.

One man, a bank robber, escaped and swam all the way to the mainland. Then someone saw him, and he was caught and sent back to Alcatraz.

Alcatraz was a tough prison. Eight prisoners were murdered by other prisoners in the twenty-eight years it was a prison.

Houdini

Some people make a living out of escaping. They make it into an "art" for the stage. Harry Houdini (say "who-DEE-nee") is the most famous escape artist of all time.

He could escape from:

- handcuffs
- ropes
- chains
- straitjackets

Houdini could take his arm bones out of his shoulder sockets to get out of straitjackets. Then he popped them back in!

Scotland Yard

For one trick, Houdini was locked into Scotland Yard in 1890, the main building of the British police. He was naked so that he couldn't hide any tools.

He got out.

How Did He Do It?
He cut a tiny flap into the hard dead skin on his foot and hid a little watch spring inside. Once he was inside Scotland Yard, he used the spring to pick all the locks. He threw away the spring before he went outside and amazed all the police officers there.

A famous London bank told Houdini he would never get out of their safe. Houdini did!

His wife passed a small piece of wire into his mouth as she kissed him for good luck!

1915: Houdini escaped from a straitjacket while he was hanging upside down from a building.

2003: Shahid Malik made "Houdini's Escape" even more dangerous by setting the rope on fire.

Great Escapes

Henry "Box" Brown

Henry Brown was a slave in Virginia in the nineteenth century. White farmers in the southern states wanted to keep slaves to work for them. Some people in the northern states wanted slaves to be freed.

In 1849, Henry Brown squeezed himself into a small wooden box. He got two of his friends to send the box to an antislavery group in a northern city. When he got there, he joined the group and fought to stop slavery!

The journey took more than a day. Brown had water in his box, and there were air holes. Even though "right side up with care" was written on the side of the box, for some of the journey he was upside down.

The Berlin Wall

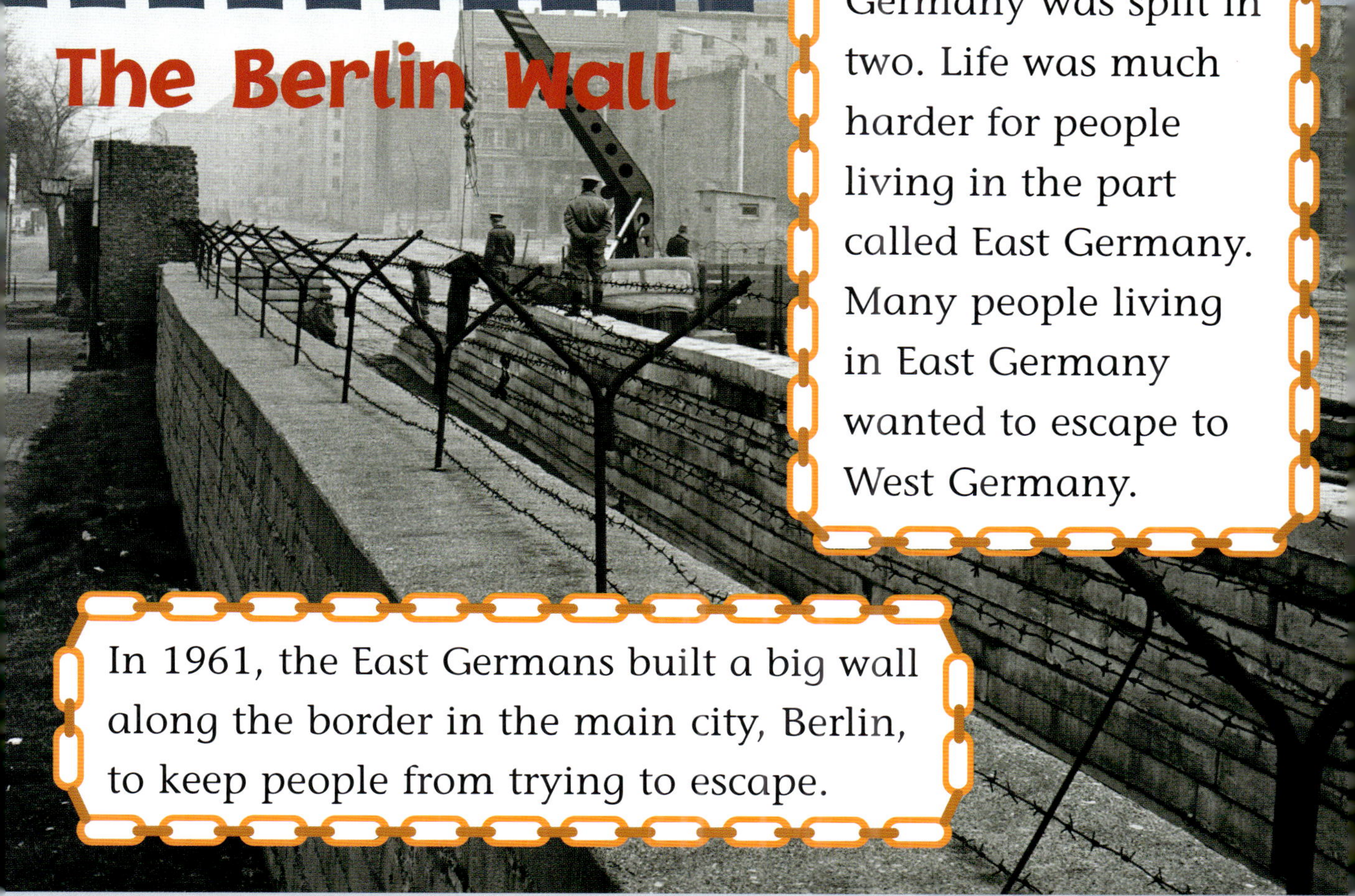

After World War II, Germany was split in two. Life was much harder for people living in the part called East Germany. Many people living in East Germany wanted to escape to West Germany.

In 1961, the East Germans built a big wall along the border in the main city, Berlin, to keep people from trying to escape.

People still escaped across the wall in many ways. Some people strapped themselves under cars. In 1964, fifty-seven people escaped through a tunnel that started in a bathroom in East Berlin. The tunnel was 43 feet (13 m) underground and 476 feet (145 m) long. It came out in West Berlin.

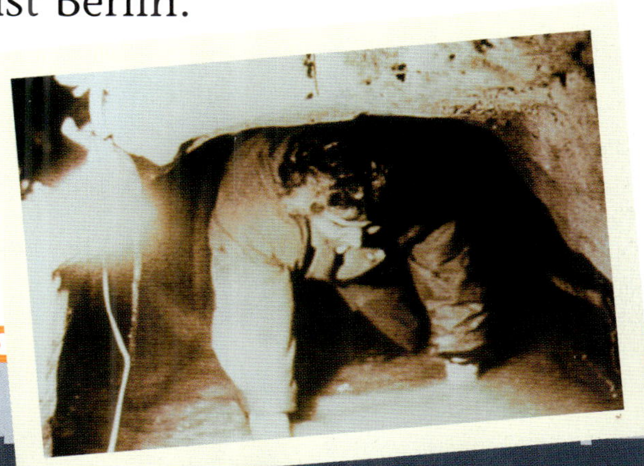

Aliens in the U.S.

Plants and animals that have "escaped" and live in the wild are called aliens.

In the United States alone, there are 7,000 aliens! Animals escape from farms, zoos, and homes. Plants escape from gardens and farms. Aliens also catch rides on boats and planes from other parts of the world. Aliens can cause lots of damage to the environment, and even to people.

In the 1800s, a Florida gardener brought water hyacinths to his home. They escaped.

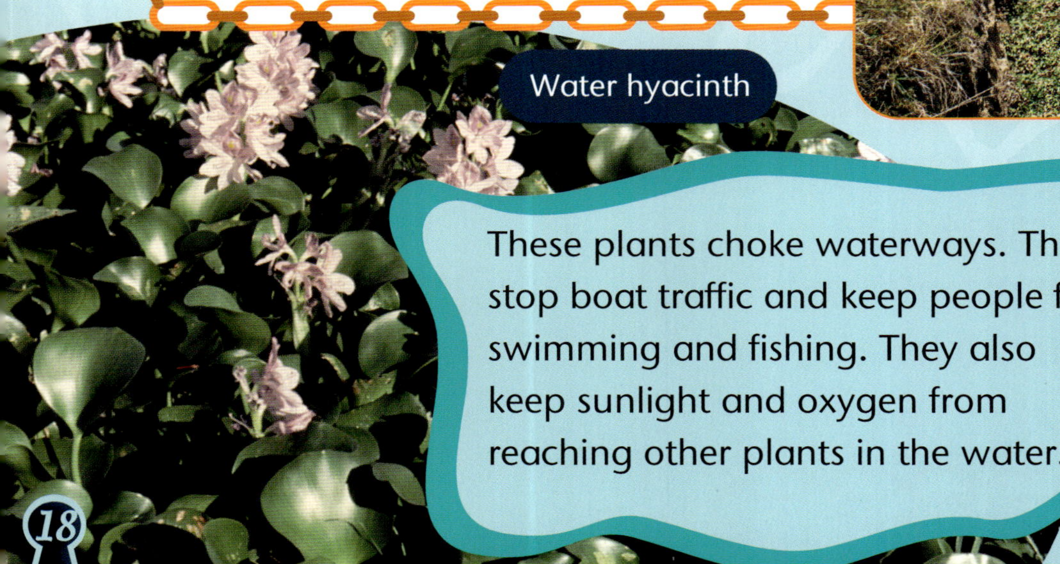

Water hyacinth

These plants choke waterways. They stop boat traffic and keep people from swimming and fishing. They also keep sunlight and oxygen from reaching other plants in the water.

People once used this plant to decorate their gardens. Now it grows all over the U.S.

Japanese knotweed

It is so strong, it can even push through concrete!

Scotch thistle can be so big and spiny that people, livestock, and even wildlife cannot walk through it. This means that no one can use the land.

It can grow up to 8 feet (2.5 m) tall.

Scotch thistle

Animals

These animals are aliens. They have escaped and are now wild. Alien animals can harm the environment.

In some parts of the U.S., the Chinese mitten crab has become a huge threat to other water animals. It is now illegal to bring them to this country.

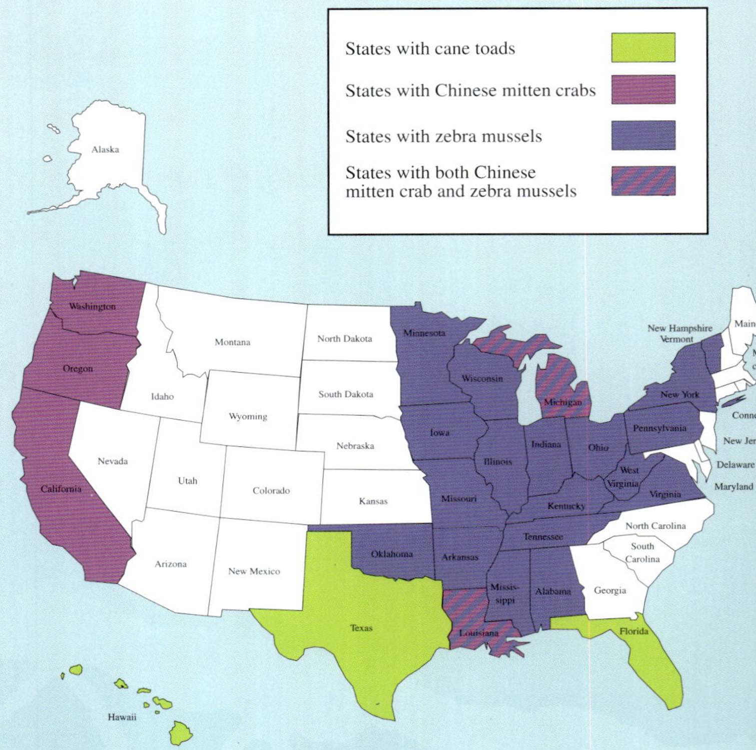

Zebra mussels came from the Caspian Sea. In the U.S., they live mostly in rivers and lakes. They block drinking-water pipes, pollute water, and damage power stations.

Cane toads were brought to Hawaii and Florida to eat sugar cane beetles. Yet cane toads have poison in their skin glands that kills animals when they try to eat the toads. Without other animals eating them, the number of cane toads keeps growing.

The nutria (say "NEW-tree-uh") is a South American rodent that likes to swim. In the U.S., nutria escaped from fur farms. They like marshes, and destroy riverbanks and dam areas by digging burrows. They have also damaged huge areas of marshland by eating the plants that grow there.

Some animals escape but get caught again! They are not aliens – they did not live wild for very long.

A chimpanzee escaped from London Zoo, jumped on a bus, and bit a passenger before it was caught.

MBCs

MBC means "mystery big cat." On the island of Maui in Hawaii, people have been claiming to see MBCs since the late 1980s. Scientists have been called in to help figure out if people really are seeing big cats.

Some people think that the big cats are really one cat that escaped and now lives wild.

Scientists found a sample of cat fur, but they're still not positive what kind of cat the MBC is.

The MBC might be a jaguar, leopard, or mountain lion.

A big cat is any cat bigger than a domestic cat. Big cats are not a natural animal in Hawaii. They can do lots of damage, and it is even illegal to have them as pets.

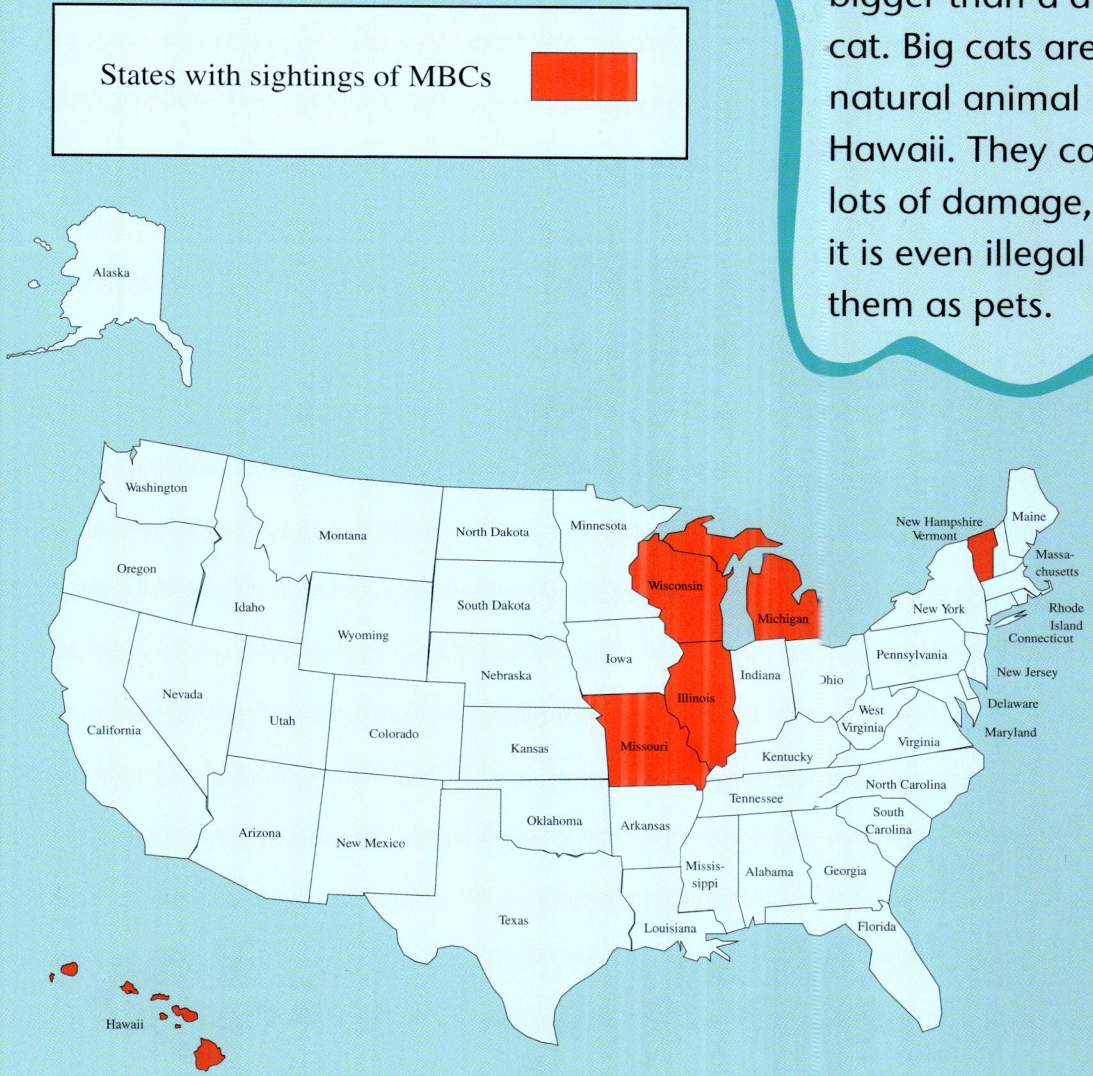

Would you kill “alien” animals and plants if they damaged wildlife or the environment where you live? How far back would you go? Horses came to North America in the sixteenth century.

Escape the Maze

Can you escape from this maze?

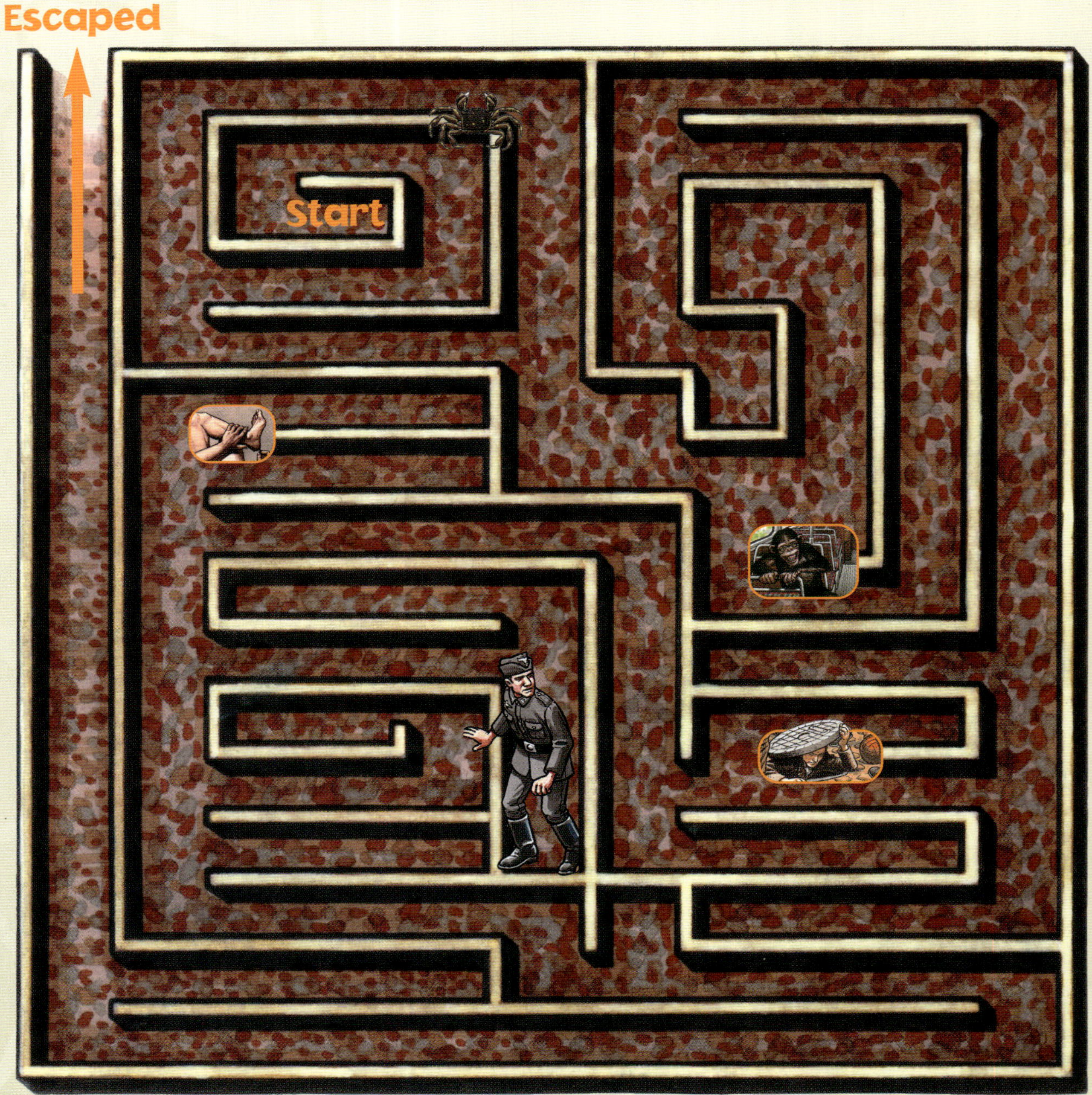